LEARNING TO TEACH

LEARNING TO TEACH

Responsibilities of Student Teachers & Cooperating Teachers

Carley Meyer Schweinberg

ROWMAN & LITTLEFIELD
Lanham • Boulder • New York • London

Published by Rowman & Littlefield
A wholly owned subsidiary of The Rowman & Littlefield Publishing Group, Inc.
4501 Forbes Boulevard, Suite 200, Lanham, Maryland 20706
www.rowman.com

Unit A, Whitacre Mews, 26-34 Stannary Street, London SE11 4AB

British Library Cataloguing in Publication Information Available

Library of Congress Cataloging-in-Publication Data Available

ISBN 978-1-4758-2030-0 (cloth)
ISBN 978-1-4758-2031-7 (pbk.)
ISBN 978-1-4758-2032-4 (e-book)

∞™ The paper used in this publication meets the minimum requirements of
American National Standard for Information Sciences—Permanence of Paper
for Printed Library Materials, ANSI/NISO Z39.48-1992.

Printed in the United States of America

CONTENTS

PREFACE

You've likely heard the phrase "children are our future." If that is the case, then our student teachers are our *near* future! As teachers we are the guardians and shepherds to the young minds that will someday cure diseases, develop new energy sources, and take care of both the young and old.

It is our sometimes unappreciated and unglamorous duty to prepare our students to be both good workers and good citizens. In order to do that, we need to connect and collaborate with students so they see the work that we do together as meaningful and a reflection of themselves.

And it is the job of student teachers and cooperating teachers to connect in the same way with each other so that they are mutually beneficial. When cooperating teachers support their student teachers, and the student teachers in turn grow into successful teachers, students win.

Student teachers, also called teacher interns and pre-service teachers, need to feel safe and supported throughout their placements so that they are able to learn from and assist their cooperating teachers, also referred to as mentor teachers or supervising teachers, while growing as future educators.

Once paired up, a cooperating teacher and a student teacher may find that they are similarly suited for each other. They may have similar personalities, come from similar backgrounds, have common interests, or share a similar style of teaching. However, mentor teachers and teacher interns may find that they are not very much alike. If that happens, their relationship may start off with suspicions or false beliefs.

The supervising teacher may surmise that this particular teacher intern won't be as effective as a former intern. The supervising teacher may imagine that his or her pre-service teacher isn't prepared or very dedicated to his or her future profession.

A student teacher who doesn't immediately see eye to eye with his or her cooperating teacher may think that his or her mentor teacher is out of touch or snobby. The pre-service teacher may feel that if he or she isn't good enough in their supervising teacher's eyes, then he or she won't be good enough to teach, period.

Even when the cooperating and student teacher are similar, it can be troublesome if early, unfounded expectations come into play. A mentor teacher may judge that his or her teacher intern is wholly prepared and needs less guidance and feedback since he or she is "just like me." The supervising teacher may treat the pre-service teacher more like an old friend than a teacher intern.

The student teacher might feel as though he or she isn't getting enough constructive criticism—or the opposite, feel like he or she is "perfect" and prematurely believe that he or she is ready to handle the class solo.

Through my not-so-distant experiences as a student teacher and now as a cooperating teacher I have seen how vital a meaningful relationship is to a teacher intern and mentor teacher pair. The way the two "click" and collaborate is the first necessary building block to constructing a positive student teaching experience. Without a strong foundation, it is difficult to develop the trust that is necessary to build up a resilient and engaging student teacher.

Learning about each other as teachers is often a good place to start a professional educator relationship. For examples of how to start a dialogue, see appendix A–C.

Just like our students, pre-service teachers enter our schools with different personalities, backgrounds, and skill sets. I've observed student teachers ranging from quiet to outgoing, from loaded with experience to little exposure to teaching, and from lots of out-of-school commitments to very few other responsibilities. None of these items is an indicator of success or failure in the teaching realm. All pre-service teachers have the ability to be successful. For an outline of skills student teachers should possess when entering their placement, see appendix D.

Mentor teachers come to the table with an even longer list of variables and experiences. Some cooperating teachers have taught for decades, other just a few years. Some have taken courses and studied texts about improving their ability to mentor student teachers, and others have no training. Some supervising teachers wish to be a cooperating teacher so that they have "additional help" in the classroom, while others feel the responsibility to "pay it forward" to the next generation of teachers, just as their teacher role models had done for them.

How a pre-service teacher enters his or her student teaching placement is nowhere near as important as how they exit. Coming into a placement with initial deficits (which *no* teacher intern is without) doesn't mean a student teacher cannot mature into an effective educator. Mentor teachers need to remember that regardless of their past training or lack thereof (see desired skills outline in appendix E), it is their guidance, support, and respect that will drive their teacher interns to become the best professional educators they can be.

If student teachers and cooperating teachers understand their roles and responsibilities to each other and to the students they are teaching, they will more than likely cultivate a respectful, positive, and collaborative working relationship. With a healthy, empathic relationship the mentor teacher will see his or her teacher intern as helpful in benefiting the students rather than a hindrance in the classroom, and in turn the pre-service teacher will become confident and productive.

Future communities, schools, families and students will reap the benefits of the well-prepared student teachers that cooperating teachers now support. Mentor teachers—nurture the intellects and spirits of the pre-service teachers you serve, and you will serve and stimulate countless young minds for years to come.

ACKNOWLEDGMENTS

To my husband, daughter, parents, mother-in-law, father-in-law, and family and friends for your positive encouragement, advice, support, and love.

To my principal, university professors, colleagues, and student teachers for your valuable input and inspiration.

And to my students and their families for allowing me the privilege of working with you!

INTRODUCTION

Young men and women who wish to become teachers throw themselves into their student teaching placements, trying their hand at the profession they have dreamed about and hope to be a part of someday soon.

Teacher interns hope they are fulfilling their duties to their mentor teachers and students, but how they communicate with their supervising teachers takes a backseat to course work, mandated assessments, and other requirements throughout their final year of university teacher training.

Teachers who agree to be supervising teachers do so because they believe they have something to pass on to new teachers. They have a desire to reinvest and give back to a profession they are passionate about.

Cooperating teachers want to learn how to be the best mentor they can be, but there is hardly enough time in the day to plan, prepare, teach their students, let alone spend time on preparing how to best serve their student teachers.

Mentor teachers and pre-service teachers have plenty on their plates and cannot spend additional hours of their time navigating a phonebook-thickness text for ideas! What cooperating teachers and student teachers need is something *simple*, pragmatic, casual, and concise to get their relationship off on the right track. This books aims to fulfill those needs.

Within this text are chapters dedicated to several areas that require discussion early on in a student teaching placement. Each chapter begins with a real-world teaching scenario then continues with two viewpoints—one outlining a cooperating teacher's perspective in regards to a teacher intern, and one describing the perceptions of a student teacher to a mentor teacher. These chapters give a voice to both the supervising teacher and the pre-service teacher and help each know more about what the other is thinking and why.

Nothing in this book is earthshaking—the examples within the given chapters are thoughts that every student teacher and cooperating teacher has encountered before. The difference is, out of courtesy or fear you may not have made these thoughts known to your pre-service teacher or supervising teacher. Or you may have *thought* you have said these things, were planning on discussing them, or you may not have been able to put your thoughts into words.

To get the most out of this book, read both portions of each chapter so that you will have a better insight into developing a comfortable relationship with your student teaching counterpart as well as a better understanding of your own role.

The content of this book will only be useful if it is followed by thoughtful discussion with your student teacher or cooperating teacher. Appendix F outlines questions to discuss after reading. Have an open and honest conversation about what you read and how it pertains to your situation. Use the forms and examples in the appendixes that are applicable to your relationship and situation.

You may find that many examples within this text resonate with you, but it is also likely that you won't agree with everything. Both will prove interesting and enlightening when mentor teacher and teacher intern confer. Happy reading and cheers to a great relationship and prepared, thoughtful future teachers!

1

FEEDBACK—
CONSTRUCTIVE CRITICISM
MEETS PAT ON THE BACK

Anna completes her lesson on the phases of matter as the lunch bell rings. The students file out and Anna nervously eyes Mrs. DeBord, her cooperating teacher, as she quickly finishes jotting down notes on her observation form. Anna reflects back to the lesson—she stumbled through the experiment's "attention getter" and took twenty minutes longer to complete the activity than she had planned. The ice experiment went well, but the homework Anna had intended to pass out is still sitting on the back counter.

Anna quietly sits down at Mrs. DeBord's desk with a wounded look in her eye, but hungry for approval.

DEAR STUDENT TEACHER,

As you begin your student teaching placement, please know that it is *not* your cooperating teacher's job to teach you how to be a teacher, but rather to fine-tune the skills you already possess. You have likely already spent many hours around children, have had practice lesson planning, and you may have already spent time in a school setting to observe and teach.

Your college courses have prepared you in terms of content, but your hands-on student teaching experience will teach you how to function as a daily, in the trenches, "real deal" teacher.

Your cooperating teacher is undoubtedly excited to share his or her knowledge with you so that you can be prepared to student teach this year, and on your own once you graduate. Being your supervising teacher is a huge responsibility—to both you and the students.

This responsibility makes your cooperating teacher nervous! Your mentor teacher is your model for the duration of your placement and he or she does not want to botch your experience.

As your placement begins, your mentor needs to focus on two very important goals: preparing you to teach, and preparing the students to learn. In order to achieve those two important goals, your supervising teacher needs to set high expectations for your planning and performance.

When you and your cooperating teacher have your weekly sit-downs, he or she will be very honest about areas you need to work on in order to become an even better teacher. Constructive criticism is crucial to your development as a teacher. Your mentor teacher could simply tell you "you're doing well" or "your lesson was good," but he or she doesn't want to give you a false sense of confidence in your teaching and needs to provide you with constructive feedback that you should welcome.

No teacher—new or veteran—is going to be perfect. And don't think perfection is what you are striving for during your placement. What you should be aiming toward is doing your best, learning from your experiences, and moving on to your next challenge, while developing as a professional educator. Your successes, failures, and "ho-hum" lessons will guide your thinking and planning for future lessons.

Through your cooperating teacher's own early teaching adventures, and now as an experienced teacher, he or she has likely made many mistakes. Every teacher remembers the terrible lessons, awkward activities, and embarrassing observations better than he or she remembers the countless remarkable things he or she has done to make learning interesting and engaging for students.

Both the outstanding and the cringe-worthy experiences help shape the way all teachers teach, and have made veteran teachers the resilient educators that they are today. Mentor teachers want to pass on their knowledge and experience to you, but you have to be open to receiving it.

DEAR COOPERATING TEACHER,

Your student teacher knows that his or her role is to learn as much as possible from you and his or her placement. The experiences you provide for your intern will undoubtedly help him or her become a successful teacher (and hopefully he or she will get hired!).

The situations your pre-service teacher encounters may include working with your department or grade-level team, interacting with the families of your students, and watching you plan, prepare, and deliver lessons that are appropriate for your students. But what will be the most challenging, thrilling, and instructive will be the lessons student teachers design and teach themselves.

After teaching a lesson, some teacher interns process well out loud with their mentor teacher while reviewing the components of the completed lesson. While discussing the effectiveness of the executed activity, many pre-service teachers welcome their cooperating teachers' input. They want to see your notes and understand your suggestions.

Your student teacher likely respects your insights and observations when you meet after teaching a lesson but there *is* something some teacher interns have a tough time appreciating as much as they should— the "constructive" criticism following their lessons.

Don't get your intern wrong, he or she *doesn't* want you to spout rainbows and sunshine just to make him or her feel good, but your preservice teacher probably hates hearing about all the things he or she is doing wrong!

Student teachers aren't sure if their cooperating teachers realize how much time and energy they pour into each lesson and activity they prepare! Teacher interns spend hours tweaking their plans to best fit your requirements and are crushed or disappointed when it doesn't match your expectations.

Many student teachers' school experiences have been positive, which may have contributed to them wanting to become teachers. Your teacher intern may have earned good grades and perhaps most subjects came easily to your intern during his or her formative years. But now your pre-service teacher may feel as though he or she is hearing mostly about "areas to improve" but hardly hearing about any "strengths." Student teachers *need* positive—and specific—constructive feedback.

Just like school-age students, teacher interns need positive reinforcement to let them know that they are on the right track. Interns can't conjure up the confidence to tackle new challenges if they don't feel satisfied about the tasks that have already been attempted. They need daily encouragement to keep them going!

Many universities provide a standard form to fill out when observing student teachers, but if not, consider developing a system or a guide to follow when evaluating your student teacher. You could also use appendix G as a simple observation form. Try to keep the positives and negatives of his or her lesson at least balanced so that your intern understands that you see all the ways they are doing things "right" as well as the areas that need improvement. This lets your pre-service teacher know that you are pleased with parts of his or her progress even though there are areas to refine.

If your student teacher feels valued and successful, he or she is going to preform at a higher level and be more open to receiving criticism.

2

SLOW DOWN,
ONE THING AT A TIME

Following Jackson's lesson on Mesoamerica, Mrs. Cunningham sits down and outlines a few areas that require attention and improvement. She is happy to have seen and thought of a few recommendations that she and Jackson can discuss together. Mrs. Cunningham feels less than helpful when she has no new critiques to point out to her student teacher.

Jackson, on the other hand, looks less than pleased to hear about the list of his needed "instructional improvements." He thought he did a great job!

Jackson looks defeated and feels overwhelmed by his cooperating teacher's suggestions. Jackson feels as though there are too many "negatives" to work on before his next lesson.

DEAR STUDENT TEACHER,

Through years of experience, teachers have faced many challenges that have ended in both success and failure. Many teachers cannot count the number of times they came home discouraged or cried after a tough day of student teaching. It may even happen now as a veteran teacher from time to time!

But through the adversities teachers have encountered, experienced teachers learned to tweak their teaching. Large class size? Rearrange the room. Student with special needs? Adapt the learning space and lessons to fit his needs. Student with behavioral needs? Create an individual plan to keep her motivated and on track. Irate parent? Listen to the parent's needs and together devise a solution that works best for the student. Veteran and mentor teachers seem to have an answer to go along with almost any possible situation.

This expertise wasn't created overnight. Expert teachers have spent years honing their skills and *near*-perfecting their craft. As a situation arose, they grappled with the best way to handle it and learned from their success or failure. If a similar situation came up again, they were prepared to operate accordingly.

Cooperating teachers have learned *so much* through their teaching careers and aspire to pass on as much of that knowledge as possible so that their pre-service teachers can hopefully avoid some of the difficulties that they have encountered.

It may not feel like it now, but your student teaching semester or year is fleeting. Many mentor teachers will try to dispense as much wisdom, advice, and thoughtful, constructive criticisms as they can during the given time you have together.

The more your supervising teacher shares, the better he or she feels that you are as informed and prepared for the classroom as possible. That way your cooperating teacher knows, "I've done my job!"

DEAR COOPERATING TEACHER,

Student teachers everywhere are relieved to know that they are not the only ones who have hung their heads or shed tears of defeat following a terrible day of teaching. When a lesson goes poorly (or not 100 percent as planned), teacher interns may feel like they have failed you and themselves. It may cause them to question whether or not they have what it takes to be teachers.

Cooperating teachers enjoy sharing what they have learned over the years and their analyses of teacher interns' lessons. And pre-service teachers hope they can gain insights from their mentor teachers' knowledge and critiques. You may find yourself gushing information as it pops in your head, but be aware of how your intern is processing your comments. Some supervising teachers' stories and "thoughtful criticisms" are, yes, thoughtful, but sometimes overwhelming!

Many student teachers' main goal at this time is survival, planning and executing lessons—period. It takes lots of time and energy to accomplish just that. Teacher interns use all the focus they can muster during a lesson to simply hit the areas that they are *supposed* to be addressing within the appropriate time frame. Interns don't know if you remember your early days of teaching—*it's tough!*

Student teachers know that teaching isn't just planning and delivering lessons, but many can't handle focusing their attention on much more than that early on in their placement.

As teacher interns become more confident in lesson planning and teaching, they can start taking baby steps into controlling pacing, "using the room," exploring voice inflection and intonation, embedding assessment, and all the other components you experienced teachers seem to do simultaneously.

Try to gradually immerse student teachers into the teaching process and transition them into full-time teaching with support and empathy. Student teachers want to learn it all and do it all, but first they need to digest one piece of effective instruction before they bite off another. Just as young students cannot learn to write without first learning their letters, pre-service teachers cannot become master teachers before learning and practicing teaching basics.

③

APPRECIATE YOUR STUDENTS

Matthew wraps up his first tumultuous week of student teaching, tired and reeling from a new school, new schedule, a new cooperating teacher, and dozens of new students! Matthew feels as though he created good connections with many of his young learners but some students seem apathetic or don't appear to like him at all. Matthew tries not to worry—it's only been a week—but he can't shake the dreadful thought that he won't be a successful teacher intern if his students dislike him.

DEAR STUDENT TEACHER,

Every fall teachers all over the country receive a new mixed-bag of personalities in their classes. Students can be shy, outgoing, hardworking, laid back, mischievous, lazy, or gifted (or a combination!). In your class you may find yourself drawn to a few students right away—perhaps those students who remind you of yourself, or students who are sweet, soft-spoken, and thoughtful. You'll learn to love the class clown and enjoy his or her silliness.

But there will be students in our class that don't make you laugh. They may not remind you of yourself. These students may be cold, aloof, or even rude. These students may include a pupil with a name that is difficult to pronounce, a student with an IEP, or the seemingly shy student that keeps to him or herself. You may find yourself interacting with these students less often than the others.

Every teacher has encountered this scenario, and it's tricky. We all know that each of these children is someone's whole world—but you don't understand them like their families might. You may try to initiate contact with a student by smiling or striking up a conversation because you feel like you should, but even kindergartners can tell whether you are genuine or not.

If you think back to your own school experiences, you'll remember the teachers you liked and those you weren't so fond of. And chances are the teachers you didn't especially care for were the teachers that you believed didn't like you.

In those teachers' classes you probably didn't try as hard nor perform as well as you could. You may have suspected that the teachers in question didn't think you were very smart or hardworking so that became a self-fulfilled prophesy. What a horrible way to spend one whole year of your life!

Now think about the children in class that you don't initially "click with"—do you want them to feel that way? Of course not.

The student(s) in question may be new to the community, may speak a different language/have a different culture at home, have a difficult home life, be painfully shy, or they may be bullied, have a medical issue or learning disability. In older students the problems could include harassment, physical or sexual assault, grappling with sexual identity, or homelessness.

You need to be a positive, compassionate person in your students' lives and prove to them that you really care. Once a student knows you genuinely care, he or she will be capable of becoming the student you knew he or she could be.

How students feel about school, their classmates, and their teachers has a direct connection with their academic success. The more a student cares about his teachers and fellow students, the more he will care about what he is learning in class. If a teacher puts effort into helping all students feel at ease, the students' chances are much better for performing at their best.

How do you do this? Truly care about your students. Help each feel comfortable and safe while in your classroom. Talk to your students about nonschool related interests. *Really* listen when they share things with you, remember what they say, and follow up. Admit when you are wrong. Reassure your students when they are upset and congratulate them on their successes. Smile.

Smile when your students enter the room; give them a wink or a nod when they leave. Be prepared to teach at your best each day and your students will see how much you *love* being a teacher—and how much you *love* being *their* teacher!

Prove to your students that they are important to you, show it and say it every day. When you put in the effort to help and care for all students, they feel connected to you. If your students feel loved, they love you back (even if they don't show it!). What a wonderful way to spend a year!

DEAR COOPERATING TEACHER,

It is interesting for your student teacher to be on the other side of the desk for his or her first day of school. As a school-age student, your teacher intern sized up his or her teachers and figured out pretty fast what the teachers were like, and what he or she could (or could not) get away with in class. Now your intern is the one being scrutinized by their students!

As the students in your class get a read on you and your pre-service teacher as their new teachers, your student teacher is busy watching and listening to the students.

Your teacher intern may recognize some students as "sweet" or "funny" right away. He or she will notice the "smart" and "quiet" students and the "tough but loveable" characters in the classroom. But there will be a few students who may not stick out right away as one "type" of student or another. These students may remain a mystery.

Your student teacher might not know how to connect with some of these students. They may be cold and unfriendly. Perhaps these students act like they don't care about school, or care about much of anything.

Your teacher intern may feel like those students don't like him or her, which may cause him or her anxiety. If I were a good teacher, your intern may think, all the students would like me, right?

Wrong! Students come to school with different personalities and carrying different loads and burdens. How a student responds to a teacher, especially at the beginning of the year, has more to do with the student than the teacher.

Most students—whether a teacher is their favorite or not—respect their teachers, but there are exceptions. If a student feels overlooked, misunderstood, or unloved, he or she may remain shy and disconnected. Or the student may bring attention to the inequality he or she feels by refusing to complete schoolwork, treating teachers and fellow students rudely, or hurting others through words or actions.

Some quiet or "unfriendly" seeming students may aspire to fly under the radar and go unnoticed. Those students may not strive for attention and "get lost" in the daily shuffle. Try to think like an engaging, observant teacher and think of ways to read them in the classroom.

Your student teacher may encounter students like this, or may encounter the opposite student. Especially in older grades, pre-service teachers may find that some students like them too much! A student may be too friendly, get too personal, and cross the teacher-student line. Your intern has to tread lightly—he or she wants to maintain a professional, respectful relationship without hurting delicate feelings.

Your student teacher may be ill-equipped to handle these awkward and potentially damaging student situations. Your teacher intern may be confused about how some students act—it could be a far cry from his or her own school experiences.

Your intern may have to adjust his or her way of thinking. Not everyone grew up the same way—good or bad—and your pre-service teacher shouldn't set up expectations based on a limited point of view.

Help your student teacher understand that every student is different, and differences are not only expected, but also embraced. Instill in your teacher intern the concepts of equity versus equality. All students need different types and amounts of support to help them be at their best.

And most importantly, be the example of how to treat students with love and respect to earn it in return.

4

GET A LIFE!

After hearing Mrs. Jameson lamenting the fact that report card grades are due soon and the new writing assessment needs to be planned, Ronaldo is surprised to hear that his cooperating teacher has a weekend shopping trip planned with her family.

"How can she possibly go away for the weekend?" Ronaldo asks himself. "I can barely fit in time to sleep with all my schoolwork and I'm not even a full-time teacher yet!"

DEAR STUDENT TEACHER,

During your student teaching placement you will eat, sleep, and breathe teaching. You will observe and teach in a school, then attend your college courses and discuss teaching. You will spend time out of class working on teaching assignments and then you will likely spend countless additional hours just talking about, you guessed it—teaching—with fellow student teachers and other friends and family.

Mercy! The life of a pre-service teacher is long and often unvaried. From sunup to sundown, month in and month out, interns prepare for their careers as teachers by immersing themselves in their studies and placements. As a student teacher you will learn a lot, and will understand—firsthand—the rigors and time commitment it takes to become a teacher.

It would be easy to lock yourself away and focus only on your teaching, emerging only for class and fast food. It is, after all, what you are planning on doing with the rest of your life! However, like any healthy relationship, a balance should exist between your personal life and your studies to make it all work.

Most cooperating teachers have various interests or passions that keep them busy outside of school. Gardening, cooking, exercising, reading, and seeing friends and family are all great ways to relax and focus energies on other areas of life. Teaching, planning, and grading take up so much of teachers' time; they need to express themselves in other facets of their lives to remain well balanced and happy. Variety is the spice of life!

Try to think like a seasoned teacher who knows you need to take breaks, whether it's for a few minutes, hours, for the afternoon, or even for a few days (gasp!) to focus on different interests or activities. Taking a step back from your studies is healthy for you, physically, mentally, and emotionally.

Distance can also provide clarity to a problem you've been worrying about. Can't figure out how to fit your upcoming unit within your mentor teacher's schedule? Go for a bike ride and it may fall into place when you aren't concentrating on it. Having trouble finding the words to say to an unmotivated student? Grab a snack and take a walk downtown. The right words might pop into your head.

Do not feel like you aren't a "serious" student teacher if you take time away from your courses and placement workload for a little fun or relaxation. If you think back to your favorite teachers or professors, you may remember that they loved to play the guitar, sang with the choir, or ran races just for the health of it. Those interesting, multifaceted teachers were probably enjoyable to be around and could connect with students about various interests.

Having a variety of hobbies and outlets is a great way to unwind. It is also a good way to prove to yourself that you are capable of doing other things well—not just teaching!

So next time you're feeling stressed, tired, or burned out, stop what you're doing and go do something else. Your brain and nerves will thank you!

DEAR COOPERATING TEACHER,

Student teaching involves a whirlwind of emotions. Student teachers feel happy, then sad, confused, then elated, over the many small victories and obstacles that crop up in their student teaching placements.

The more successful a teacher intern feels, the harder he or she works to maintain the pace and current level of performance. The more failure and setbacks an intern encounters, the more behind he or she feels and the harder he or she works to stay afloat. Either way, student teachers are constantly pushing themselves to do their best for their cooperating teachers, students, professors, and themselves.

With the time it takes to prepare for class and school placements, pre-service teachers have little time to socialize, exercise, or even play on their smart phones! *You* may have time for fun after school or on the weekends, but your intern goes from school to more school or home to a huge pile of homework!

Student teachers never feel caught up with all the work they need to complete as they straddle their two lives as a college student and as a budding teacher. They still feel like college students—young and adventurous—but the numerous duties of looming adulthood and their future career may stop them from participating in the activities they love. There just isn't enough time!

You can do your part to ensure that your hardworking teacher intern gets a break every now and then. Thinking of sending your intern home with papers to grade or lamination to cut out? Give him or her the night off every so often.

You want your student teacher to understand teachers' "real" day-to-day lives, but keep in mind that he or she isn't being paid and needs time to relax and have some fun!

5

PLAN TO PLAN

Sarah and her cooperating teacher, Mr. Weldy, convene during their weekly, agreed upon, meeting time on Monday morning. But during the meeting, Sarah says she hasn't decided which duty she'd like to take over next and she left her weekly goal sheet at her apartment. So Tuesday morning the pair sits down again to go over a few forms and co-plans an upcoming lesson.

On Wednesday Sarah remembers she needs an observation form filled out, and then requests that Mr. Weldy review a stack of lesson plans for the following week.

After receiving an e-mail later that day, Sarah anxiously asks her co-operating teacher to find time to meet with her university professor on Thursday afternoon. By the end of the week Mr. Weldy is "done" with his student teacher's meetings!

DEAR STUDENT TEACHER,

Sometimes teachers' days are mapped out like an agenda in a series of meetings. Teachers go to IEP meetings, staff meetings, and grade-level or department meetings. Teachers meet with parents, students, and monitor after-school sports and clubs. During nonschool hours teachers follow a personal agenda—haircuts, book club, intramural soccer, and dinner dates. Teachers are an organized, schedule-loving bunch!

And most teachers aim to keep it that way. Teachers are methodical planners, and each has a system—of some sort—that he or she follows. Maybe every Monday morning before school a teacher gathers the reference books she will use for the week or during his morning break every Thursday, a teacher writes his weekly newsletter.

Teachers thrive on routine just like students. They like knowing what needs to be accomplished and have a plan for going about completing it. *Then you showed up!*

Your presence threw everything slightly off-kilter and your cooperating teacher no longer has the same routines and "system" he or she had before you began your placement. Don't blame yourself—you didn't do anything wrong. Your mentor teacher signed up to be your supervisor, so it is his or her responsibility to make necessary adjustments. But you can help make the process as pain free as possible.

Treat your sit-down chats with your cooperating teacher as a scheduled, weekly meeting. Prepare for it like you would a meeting with a parent or a professor. Know what you want to ask, discuss, or complete during this time. Together decide on the agenda for your meetings and what you will focus on each time.

When you consolidate the time it takes to discuss completed lessons, observations, and questions, you and your cooperating teacher will be able to spend more break time and preps to prepare for class—a win-win!

Student teachers arrive to their placements with (many!) forms from their university. Use your time together to fill them out as a team. Look at your calendars together for upcoming assignments and observations, and plan accordingly. Also discuss how you want to handle "pop-up" meetings that may come up throughout the week.

Your weekly meetings will change as the semester or year progresses. What you discuss will evolve, as you take over more and more of the daily schedule from your supervising teacher. You might use your meeting time to co-plan rather than fill out forms.

Respect your mentor teacher's time and be sure to thank him or her for dedicating time and energy to helping you on your path to becoming a successful educator. You and your cooperating teacher may end up looking forward to your weekly gatherings, rather than seeing it as one more meeting to check off the list.

DEAR COOPERATING TEACHER,

Student teachers have a lot on their plate as they navigate a new school, new classroom, new students, and a new cooperating teacher (you!). On top of the time commitment and workload you have planned for your teacher intern, your intern has an equal-size load from his or her professors.

Pre-service teachers have to fulfill the demands that are placed on them as students and as teachers. Through their college courses they complete reading assignments, projects, and group work that they hope will transfer into their teaching placement.

Your student teacher is likely excited to have time to sit down and talk with you about his or her coursework and the engaging activities you teach. Your pre-service teacher doesn't want to waste your time but is bound to have many questions, and will want to pick your brain to help develop interesting and relevant lessons.

Student teachers walk a fine line between wanting to take a leadership role in their placements, and wanting direction from you. Especially toward the beginning of their placements, teacher interns may want guidance as to their role in the classroom each week. As interns become comfortable in their planning and teaching, they may want to outline their own goals and set agendas that work for their needs.

Assignments are bound to pop up and plans may change, so your student teacher may request to confer with you during a spur-of-the-moment additional meeting (or two, or three!) each week. Be patient and help quell their fears, but also don't be afraid to say, "We will talk about it later!"

6

NAVIGATING
PROFESSIONAL RELATIONSHIPS

Megan is in uncharted territory. Parent teacher conferences are only a few days away and she has no idea what to do. Megan's cooperating teacher, Mr. Harr, is taking most of the responsibility for leading the conferences, but asked Megan to prepare a few things to say about each student. Megan isn't afraid to talk to her students, and she feels confident in how she has taught so far, but she is terrified about talking to parents!

Mr. Harr seems so nonchalant about the impending conferences while Megan is a bundle of nerves. "What should I say?" she worries to herself, "And what should I wear?"

DEAR STUDENT TEACHER,

Every family is different. Families raise their children with their set of values and their own idea of what "normal" means to them. Geography, economic status, ethnicity, and religion play large roles in a family's lifestyle. As you begin your placement you may see that the school culture and families are similar to schools you attended or perhaps they are very different.

If you find that your school is different, think about why. Is the school more or less affluent than where you went to school? Is the student body more diverse? Less diverse? Do you feel comfortable? Out of place?

Student teachers are thrown into placements where they may not initially feel at ease. It is your job (along with your cooperating teacher's help) to shed light on what is unfamiliar or intimidating to you. Real growth happens when you are out of your comfort zone and have to adapt to a new environment!

Research the neighborhoods around the school and the families that live there. What do parents around here do for a living? Are there any major employers in the area? Are the families similar in terms of socio-economic status?

Once you learn about where you are and how you fit into this new environment, you'll get a better sense of your students and mentor teacher's colleagues and better understand the school culture and the families you serve.

Talking to parents is often difficult for many pre-service teachers. You have learned so much in your education courses about the best practices in teaching, but have rarely learned about the best practices in talking to families! But you don't have to be an expert when speaking with the families of students for the first time, or any time.

The first and only rule is to listen more and talk less. Your students' parents usually understand their children better than all of their teachers combined. So listen to what they have to say before you share about their students.

Maintain eye contact, stand or sit confidently or sit side by side and allow the parents to lead the discussion. Nod as they speak, take down notes, and interject when it is appropriate. Stay positive, and share the good you are seeing along with any negatives that you may need to bring to their attention. Be specific with your examples and have schoolwork or data ready to support what you are describing.

Parents feel connected and valued by their child's teachers when the teachers "know" their child. If you are attentive to their questions and concerns and suggest respectful solutions that are appropriate for their individual student, the parents will probably be your allies all school year.

However, some parents may not be interested in being your ally—rather, they may come to a meeting upset or combative. Teachers need to be thick-skinned and prepared to discuss the student's progress—not the student—so the communication is less personal and more objective. This can ease potentially defensive parents' attitudes and push them to see the facts in their student's academic development.

The school culture applies to staff as well as families and students. Get to know the makeup of the staff and teachers that you work with directly. Learn about staff members as teachers and as people. Interact with staff at lunch, during meetings, and at other appropriate times.

Ask about staff members' positions with the school, their personal lives, including their families, hobbies, and interests. You can share about yourself and your family, friends, and what you do outside of school. As you get to know the staff, you will feel more comfortable around them and they will be relaxed around you.

But be cognizant of what you share—the teacher who is a single mother on a tight budget may not want to hear about your new Lexus or tropical spring-break plans. Be aware that no one wants to hear inappropriate stories about your exciting weekend at downtown bars! Remember that you are in a professional work environment and keep in mind that the teachers at your placement are not your college buddies. Know your audience and school community and be respectful.

Be yourself but also keep in mind that this placement is not your job—you have yet to be hired. You are a guest in the school and need to be an ambassador for your university. Also remember that your cooperating teacher's colleagues could end up being excellent references or contacts for a future position. You could even be considered for a position in the same school or district that you student teach in.

Think of student teaching as one long, elaborate job interview. You are constantly watched, scrutinized, and "under the microscope" by teachers, administrators, and staff. Give them your best effort as they "check you out"!

Also be mindful of the new relationships you bring to your school. Your mentor teacher, school support staff, and principal may not be familiar with your university professor or site coordinator. Introduce your college professors so that your cooperating teacher and the other staff you work with are all on comfortable terms.

Be sure to think of others, listen well, and keep questions and comments considerate. You'll learn more from everyone you encounter by using your ears rather than your mouth!

DEAR COOPERATING TEACHER,

Many student teachers come to their student teaching placement after having worked in a variety of places with students from different backgrounds. Many universities require a set number of clinical hours working with children or young adults through day care, tutoring, church groups, camp counseling, and as teacher's aides.

Teacher interns may already have a level of comfort working with students; however, connecting with parents and other teachers and staff in a school setting can be a whole different experience!

The mothers, fathers, and caregivers of students expect a lot from their children's teachers, and interns may feel ill equipped to answer parents' questions and live up to each families' expectations.

Why do student teachers feel nervous about reaching out to families? Quite simply—lack of experience! Teacher interns haven't been in the habit of talking with students and their families, while veteran teachers have had years of practice.

Many of the teachers in our schools have been teaching for a while. They are from an older (and perhaps wiser!) generation and communicate differently. Experienced teachers are often comfortable striking up conversations in the workroom with new staff, substitutes, and visitors. They call parents with concerns, and send handwritten notes home with students—tasks that can be intimidating to some student teachers.

Pre-service teachers want to get to know the staff and the families of their students, but need help learning the intricacies of these types of communication since they may have little experience in that area.

Assist your student teacher by introducing him or her to staff members. Tell your teacher intern each staff members' name and what they do at the school. Utilize appendixes H or I (whichever is appropriate) in your placement as a "get to know you" activity. It will be easier for your intern to talk to someone they already know in the teacher's lounge, during morning lineup, or at assemblies, if they don't have to initiate conversation for the first time on his or her own.

Invite your student teacher to staff meetings, school functions, and events. Send home a letter, pamphlet, or get-to-know you e-mail about your teacher intern to the families of the students you teach. Better yet, have your intern do it!

Also be cognizant of how welcome your student teacher feels in your classroom. Be sure to write his or her name on the board next to yours, give him or her closet space, a desk, or a cubicle drawer or work area for personal belongings and lesson materials. Instead of using "I" when talking to students, use for example, "Miss Frederick and I." Teacher interns feel comfortable when you put in the effort to make them feel at home.

Technology continues to make everyone's lives easier and information more accessible. Many young people grew up with the Internet at their fingertips, accessing fun and useful applications and websites whenever they pleased. Perhaps mentor teachers can utilize their intern's skills in communicating on new platforms and in different ways in the classroom.

7

(SOMETIMES) MAKING YOURSELF SCARCE DURING PLANNING TIME

Ms. Fahey closes her eyes and harkens back to a few short weeks ago, when she could spend her breaks and prep-time lesson planning quietly and reading e-mails. That has changed since her student teacher, Tom, began his placement in her classroom. Ms. Fahey is getting less work completed between classes and is having to take more and more school-work home with her.

Ms. Fahey thought that hosting a student teacher would ease her teaching stressors, not add to them! She'd like more time to herself during the school day but can't think of a way to approach the subject without hurting Tom's feelings.

DEAR STUDENT TEACHER,

Whether someone is shy or outgoing, introverted or extroverted, it's a fact that everybody needs time to him or herself. Teachers need alone time to plan, run copies, answer e-mails or just sip a cup of coffee in peace. Teachers are like stage actors that are "on" all day, so it is nice to have a little downtime during a prep time or break before the next performance begins.

Once you begin your placement in your cooperating teacher's classroom, your mentor teacher loses some of his or her planning and "quiet" time to your needs in the form of questions, conversations, and paperwork. Your supervising teacher may feel like he or she is spending more of their prep time talking and doing things for you rather than doing the job he or she is paid for!

Cooperating teachers *do* understand that spending time working with their student teachers when the students are out of the room is expected; it was a given when they committed to becoming a mentor teacher. Cooperating teachers and student teachers need time together to discuss upcoming lessons and observations so that they are both on the same page with the teacher intern's course work.

However, mentor teachers cannot spend *every* break time chatting! The less prep time teachers have, the more out-of-school time expended to complete their work.

Cooperating teachers are reluctant to ask their student teachers to leave the room or to give them time alone, but it's certainly on their minds!

If you notice that your mentor teacher answers your questions quickly and with only a few words, or avoids eye contact as he or she types, locates a book, or fills out forms, it may mean, "please take a hike." Your cooperating teacher doesn't want to be rude or squash your enthusiasm, but he or she might be giving subtle hints for you to give them space.

If you notice these signs, consider what you might do to make your cooperating teacher's job less time-consuming. Ask for work to take to the teacher's workroom or work quietly in a different part of the classroom. Or take the opportunity to observe other teachers, grade levels, or classes within the school. Viewing other classrooms may yield experiences different than you've had in your supervising teacher's classroom while giving your mentor space.

Supervising teachers need time and space to think. Your cooperating teacher will appreciate your thoughtfulness and will be a happier, more attentive mentor teacher after he or she completes his or her work and drinks a cup of coffee or two in silence!

DEAR COOPERATING TEACHER,

So much happens during a single day at school. Your student teacher may observe you teach (use appendix J to get the most out of your observations) and may want to talk about your approach. Your teacher intern may teach a few classes or lessons, and then may want to pick your brain at the first chance he or she has. During "break time" conversations your intern may want immediate answers and feedback while the ideas are still fresh.

Throughout these breaks your student teacher also gets to see how a real teacher functions during his or her prep time. It's great for your pre-service teacher to see a teacher in action as you plan and prepare for the following class or for the following day.

During breaks in the day your student teacher may ask questions and share thoughts. Your teacher intern isn't *trying* to annoy you—he or she just wants to know what you are thinking and doing as you get ready for the next class or lesson.

Think of student teachers as sponges, absorbing all they see and hear. It's great for teacher interns to see the other side of teaching, the side no one saw as a student. After graduation, interns will hopefully have their own classrooms and want to have as much information logged away as possible!

Your student teacher *may* understand that you need time to yourself to work or relax without him or her around. He or she may find something quiet to do while you complete your work. But if your teacher intern doesn't understand, don't be afraid to ask.

Once your student teacher takes over the majority of the classes or subjects, he or she may need time alone to gather materials, prepare for lessons, or drink an energy drink quietly. Please watch for your intern's nonverbal cues and take the hint to get lost!

8

NO COMPLAINING RULE

After a month of student teaching, Audra is mentally and physically exhausted. She feels like she has "hit the wall" and while making copies in the teacher workroom, Audra gripes to a fellow student teacher. Together they commiserate about a few troublesome students each has in class and their collective lack of sleep.

A few teachers pass by and chime in with their own frustrations. Audra doesn't want to complain to her cooperating teacher, so she is happy to have other staff members to talk about a few "educator annoyances" that are driving her crazy!

DEAR STUDENT TEACHER,

No placement is perfect. Every day brings challenges—some large, some small. Troublesome students, difficult parents, and a lesson that didn't hit your learning target can contribute to stress and make you want to scream! And if not scream, then at least complain.

Complaining comes naturally to many people. You can walk into any workplace and find nurses, bartenders, construction workers, store clerks, and CEOs complaining about their jobs. Teachers are not immune. If you enter the teacher's lounge at noon, you are bound to hear grumbles about large class sizes, budget cuts, and lack of resources.

It is easy to chime in and share your own sob story about a sassy student or an upcoming evaluation. You might feel bonded to other teachers who share in the complaining. Misery loves company, but it comes at a steep price.

Negativity and pessimism breed more negativity and pessimism, and over time you may find yourself experiencing or perpetuating distrust, failure, and defeat since that is what you have come to expect from yourself and your students.

On the other hand, describing a tricky situation and seeking ways to solve it is *not* complaining; it's problem solving. Talking to a staff member about classroom management after an experience with a disrespectful student is a good way to find applicable ideas to implement in the classroom. *This* is being proactive and seeking possible solutions—not complaining.

Complaining is rehashing a past experience in an effort to drum up sympathy, competing in the "you think *that's* bad . . ." game, or bending someone's ear to serve as an outlet for irritations. Some may find this therapeutic, but it can be damaging.

Student teachers need to watch what they say, and to whom. Courtesy and confidentiality are important—when you complain about a student's behavior, or share a student's disappointing test score to someone else, you never know who could hear. Perhaps a parent is just around the corner or another student is listening to your rant.

Discipline yourself to see the good in any given situation and when problems arise, seek out solutions rather than whine and moan—take the high road and be professional. It is amazing how much better you'll feel when you don't contribute to the chorus of complaining!

DEAR COOPERATING TEACHER,

Every day school is a beehive of energy and a setting for potential problems. Will a student refuse to do his or her work? Will a professor pop in for an impromptu evaluation? Will a parent question the grading of last week's test?

Every day is exhausting and student teachers feel like the breaks and prep time away from the students allow them to share their frustrations with fellow student teachers and other teaching staff. Teacher interns don't want to be whiners, but they may feel like it's nice to know they aren't the only ones struggling!

The connections pre-service teachers make with other annoyed staff members may be comforting to them. Student teachers feel vulnerable in their new teaching experience and may flock to others who share their same vexations.

Pay attention to your intern teacher's demeanor and take note if he or she seems depressed or anxious. You may have heard the old saying "You catch more flies with a teaspoon of honey than a gallon of vinegar." Try to create an alternative option for your intern that is sweeter than the sour feelings that may have been gnawing at them.

If possible, after a rough morning take your student teacher out to lunch. Deliver a treat or write down all the ways his or her teaching has progressed so far. Ask a student to write your teacher intern a nice note. Set up observations in a different teacher's classroom so your intern can gain a different perspective. Little things can make the biggest difference.

Student teachers' frustrations with students, parents, and lessons often stem from the lack of experience they have had in a specific area or areas of teaching. Pre-service teachers' insecurities and lack of knowledge are often to blame for the "problem" in class on a given day rather than the problem situation itself, and they need help navigating the next steps.

Teacher interns will try to keep their complaining to a minimum and "vent" to safe, nonschool channels like close friends and family. But sometimes your intern will need you as a sounding board, and you will just need to listen.

CO-TEACHING:
SUPPORTING EACH OTHER

Beverly has had a successful semester student teaching in Mr. Lutes's classroom, but two weeks into her "full takeover" portion of her training, she notices that her cooperating teacher rarely leaves the room. Beverly wonders why Mr. Lutes stays in the classroom when her fellow student teacher friends report that their mentors leave them alone to teach for hours at a time.

A few weeks ago, Beverly was glad to have Mr. Lutes in the back of the classroom observing, or walking around answering students' questions. It was reassuring to her that he was there "just in case" something she had planned didn't work out.

But now Beverly feels as though she has a good handle on her teaching but is worried that her supervising teacher doesn't trust her to teach alone.

DEAR STUDENT TEACHER,

You entered your first official school in kindergarten as a student. Later you were a middle school student, then a high school student. You graduated and enrolled in a university as a college student. And now during your semester or year of student teaching you are indeed, still a student.

You are a student, learning and studying to be a teacher. Once you begin student teaching, you may get pretty good at teaching "on your own" but that doesn't necessarily mean you need to be alone to do it.

Teaching and mentoring styles vary greatly teacher to teacher, and mentor to mentor. Some supervising teachers may slowly give their student teachers responsibilities in the classroom while others stop teaching cold turkey and hand over the reins to their teacher interns all at once.

Cooperating teachers' thoughts on full takeover practices differ greatly. Some mentor teachers may want to give their student teachers room to "do their own thing" without the mentors watching, while others want to be present in the room, most of the time, in one way or another.

If you think back to your own role at the beginning of your placement, you'll remember that you were an aide of sorts for your mentor teacher. As you became familiar with the room and the routines, you supported your cooperating teacher by co-teaching with him or her before assuming full responsibility of the classroom.

Think of your mentor teacher as your coach, assessing your skills and figuring out when you are ready to work with students or "play the game."

Once you are "the" practicing teacher in the room your roles should reverse. As you take over most of the teaching, your supervising teacher can assist you. And the guidance you needed as you began student teaching shouldn't end when you take over your mentor teacher's final section or subject area. It should continue throughout your entire placement. And the only way your cooperating teacher can continue to provide suggestions is if they are present as you teach.

Student teachers continue to need and deserve support and feedback from their cooperating teachers as they assume their mentors' daily duties. Your full takeover time is the summation of your final year in college and the peak of your teacher preparation. It is arguably the time that teacher interns need the *most* support—not the least!

Keep in mind that every mentor teacher is different and that you may need to ask for your cooperating teacher's assistance in co-teaching during your full takeover training. Your mentor may be accustomed to leaving for hours at a time—it could be what his or her supervising teacher did during his or her student teaching placement. (Though that doesn't mean it was for the best.)

As the full takeover portion of student teaching progresses you may modify the role you'd like your cooperating teacher to have in the classroom. Maybe instead of observing you, your mentor teacher could work with a small group of students, or track down resources, or individually assess students as needed. That way, your mentor still has a presence in the classroom without hovering over you.

Having a new face, a new personality, and new teaching style is a lot for some students to adjust to. Knowing that their "regular" teacher is close by can put students at ease. It also reassures the students that your cooperating teacher sees and approves of how you are conducting the classroom.

Ask your mentor to support you and aid in your teaching just as you had done for him or her while you were adjusting to your new placement.

DEAR COOPERATING TEACHER,

Teachers teach what they know. They deliver lessons that they have researched, planned, and prepared especially for their current group of students and can explain the material several different ways for different learners. Teachers adjust plans and assessments to fit the needs of their students, which can dramatically shift how they teach year to year.

So then why are some cooperating teachers still mentoring their student teachers the same way year after year? Why do some mentors counsel their teacher interns the same way they were directed as young interns?

Some veteran supervising teachers feel that once a student teacher is taking over most of the teaching, it may be a good time to give him or her more freedom. And one way to give a teacher intern more independence (as they have seen) is to leave the classroom and allow him or her to teach alone.

Perhaps when you were a student teacher, you felt liberated when your cooperating teacher left the classroom. You may have felt judged and scrutinized while teaching the class in your mentor teacher's presence. The students may have seemingly responded to you better when your mentor left the room—you were "in charge" and the students knew it.

And to some degree this custom is good. Getting out of the room every so often to give your student teacher some breathing room is solid practice. However, leaving the room all day, every day for the duration of your teacher intern's full takeover time is not a suitable habit.

Your pre-service teacher *needs* you there—especially at the beginning of full takeover—and you are doing your students a disservice if you are not present for regular pockets of time. What if a lesson goes awry? What if the class gets out of control? What if your students or student teacher needs you and you're gone?

What's worse than scant feedback from a cooperating teacher following a lesson? No feedback at all. What's worse than your teacher intern "not having a true picture of teaching" on his or her own? Your intern teaching on his or her own and having no idea if he or she is on the right track. What's worse than your student teacher failing? Failing with no one there to help.

Important moments like sharing your intern's excitement of finally "getting through" to a student need to be celebrated and built upon.

You don't have to be in the room every second of the day, holding your pre-service teacher's hand and showering him or her with praise following every activity. But you need to be helpful and present often.

Co-teaching can give your student teacher the autonomy he or she desires while you maintain a presence in the classroom. Think of ways you can support rather than evaluate your teacher intern. You could act as your intern's assistant, passing out papers, checking homework, or pulling files. You can ask what your intern needs for upcoming lessons and prepare the handouts, locate materials, or run copies of a test. For additional ideas on how to support your student teacher while he or she teaches, see appendix K.

You want your student teacher to immerse him or herself in your classroom, and to have an idea of what he or she will be doing solo once he or she has a full-time teaching job. But while your teacher intern is learning the ropes, you can make his or her job a little less stressful by helping with the small stuff.

Even if you decide to be a regular presence in the classroom for your teacher intern while they take over full-time, there will be times here and there when it could be advantageous to leave the room and allow your intern to teach without you there.

If you feel like your student teacher is ready to teach without you, step out of the room for an hour every so often. If your intern is teaching something he or she is well versed in, or has taught the past two class periods the same lesson, you could probably take off. And if your pre-service teacher asks you to leave, you could trust his or her request and head for the teacher workroom.

If you are nervous about leaving your student teacher alone, set ground rules or boundaries before allowing your teacher intern to fly solo. Together, decide how often you'll leave, for how long, and how to get you back into the classroom if necessary. Discuss the parameters of what your student teacher is teaching and your expectations for both your intern and the students.

Do you want your student teacher to give you a copy of the lesson plan so you know what is being taught while you are gone? Tell him or her that. Does your teacher intern need to adhere to your behavior management system or can they try out their own? Make your preference known. Can your intern use any resource to support an activity or does he or she need to stick to the textbook or resources you use? Make that clear.

Like in any relationship or partnership, you can't be upset if your student teacher doesn't do what you want if you haven't made those expectations known. You don't expect your significant other, your parent, or your friend to read your mind (at least you shouldn't); don't expect your intern to either!

When you return to the classroom, find some time to talk to your student teacher about how his or her lesson went and how the students responded. Asking for a recap allows you to stay in the loop while providing your teacher intern with reflection time for professional growth. Reviewing the lesson will help your intern see the positives and areas for improvement in their lesson without you suggesting them at all.

Co-teaching is crucial when your student teacher is ready to take over all of your duties as the classroom teacher. Your pre-service teacher will still feel like he or she is "on my own" with your smaller supporting role in the classroom.

10

STUDENT TEACHER AS TEACHER, COOPERATING TEACHER AS STUDENT

Just recently, in accordance to new standards, Mrs. Schafer's district changed over to a new math curriculum. Mrs. Schafer has taught math the same way for years and is feeling unsure about how to make the necessary changes in her teaching. She's been doing it the "old way" for so long!

Her student teacher, David, notices his cooperating teacher's reluctance to dive into the new curriculum and dusts off the math kit on the shelf behind her desk. David decides to take the math kit home and debunk the "scary" new curriculum. He creates a "cheat sheet" outline, hitting all the new topics to be covered and writes down a few websites as references for Mrs. Schafer.

DEAR STUDENT TEACHER,

Your cooperating teacher knows a lot. He or she began teaching years ago, bright eyed and idealistic, learning everything possible about his or her grade or subject. Your mentor teacher worked hard as a new teacher, learning the ropes while planning and teaching all day, and then went home each night exhausted but happy to be slowly mastering his or her craft.

Then a year passed, then two or maybe three, and then it all changed! Suddenly writing is now taught in a new way or the math curriculum your cooperating teacher knows forward and backward is completely revised. Perhaps the grading system is being modified or he or she is now expected to administer assessments much more frequently. Before one new change can be mastered, a new "innovation" is added, then another, and another!

Teachers everywhere have heavy loads to carry. They are expected to perform more duties than teachers ever have before. Teachers are required to test their students frequently, and are evaluated more often themselves. Teachers are given more standards to address in their teaching, but aren't always given the tools to effectively do so.

But despite the additional challenges, teachers don't shy away—they embrace the changes with the time they have. Unfortunately with all of their duties taking teachers' precious time, there can be very limited time available. You CAN teach an old dog (or teacher!) new tricks, but your cooperating teacher may need some assistance to get started.

You can help your mentor teacher by lightening the load. Are teachers at your school expected to learn a new curriculum? Volunteer to research part of it for your mentor and brief him or her on it. Is your district changing grade-book programs? Look into what those changes mean to your supervising teacher and grade-level or department team.

Perhaps your cooperating teacher's school isn't making any major changes this year. Think of something you excel in that your mentor teacher is unsure of or has little experience in.

Are you great at integrating technology in your lessons? Do you connect easily and have a good rapport with special-needs students? Are you artistic and creative? Take the role of the "master" teacher and demonstrate your skill set for your cooperating teacher. Taking the lead in a new area can make you feel more confident in your teaching ability.

One reason why teachers request to be supervising teachers is to give back to their profession and pass on the benefit of their years of teaching experience to young teachers. But teachers also choose to be mentors because they view themselves as lifelong learners.

In hosting student teachers, supervising teachers get to keep abreast of recent research in their field. New teacher interns coming into their classrooms year after year expose mentor teachers to the new advances in teaching while reminding them of the idealistic, young teachers they once were.

Like a rhino and an oxpecker bird, a cooperating teacher and a student teacher can establish a reciprocal relationship that helps the other. Each benefits—in the animal kingdom the bird eats the bugs while the rhino gets the bugs off his back. In the education realm, students ultimately benefit from having two teachers working together to make their teaching the best it can be.

You have a lot to learn from your cooperating teacher, but he or she has a lot to learn from you too. Speak up, request to help, and ask to share. It will feel wonderful to help the person who has done so much to support you.

DEAR COOPERATING TEACHER,

Through observations, note taking, and teaching courses your student teacher has picked up a lot of ideas that they'd like to try out. Your teacher intern may realize that he or she may not be able to implement everything, but he or she is probably excited to put his or her education to good use!

When your student teacher tries something new or takes a lead role it can be frightening and intimidating. But it can also be exciting and a boost to his or her confidence. Nothing makes your intern feel more empowered than implementing his or her own ideas and seeing them succeed.

Your student teacher will do this frequently in the classroom while teaching students. Your teacher intern plans an activity based on the educational needs of students. What if he or she were to do this with an instructional goal for you, and even your department or grade-level team?

Ask for your student teacher's assistance with a new initiative in your building, a new resource, or with something you have seen that he or she is passionate about that could translate well into your classroom.

Maybe your pre-service teacher sees a need and knows a way to fulfill it, or has a special skill to share. Pick your student teacher's brain about the best and newest concepts he or she is learning about in college courses. Ask about the books and resources your teacher intern is reading for class and how those topics might work in your classroom.

Student teachers are in the phase of their careers when they have the most time to focus on individual growth as teachers—a stage many veteran teachers wish they could revisit every so often! Harness the information and enthusiasm your teacher intern has for his or her new field and use it to enrich your classroom and knowledge.

In the process your intern will get a shot in the arm while learning about being a valuable member of a team. Your student teacher will be pleased to not only put his or her newfound teacher knowledge to good use but also to give back to the cooperating teacher that has taught him or her so much.

⓫

DO AS I SAY, NOT AS I DO

Following Larry's lesson, Mr. Ramos lists a few areas for improvement including "remember to include a 'wrap up' before your lesson's completion." Larry agrees that he needs to work on ending his lessons with a review about the information he presented.

But the next day, while observing his cooperating teacher, Larry can't help but notice that Mr. Ramos forgets to "wrap up" his science lesson! Then Mr. Ramos does it again the next morning after reader's workshop, and again a few days later after a math activity! Larry feels that it is unfair to require him to do something his cooperating teacher can't regularly accomplish.

DEAR STUDENT TEACHER,

No one is perfect. No teacher is perfect. You are not perfect. Your lessons will not be perfect. No matter how hard you study, research, and prepare there will always be at least one thing you can improve upon. When teaching, you will always wrap up a lesson thinking, "I wish I had remembered to do *that!*"

After you have been in your student teaching placement a while, your cooperating teacher will likely take notes and jot down examples of the things you say and do when you teach. Your mentor teacher will applaud your successes but will also point out areas in which to improve. Listening to the positives and critiques and taking time to process both will make your future lessons even better.

Back when your supervising teacher was in the midst of student teaching, he or she got a big dose of constructive feedback every time he or she taught a lesson. Once your mentor teacher was teaching on his or her own, your mentor was given suggestions to further refine his or her craft.

But your mentor teacher is imperfect too. Your cooperating teacher has had a great deal of experience teaching and will notice issues in your instruction that you will probably not. However, when your mentor teaches, you may notice that he or she doesn't always practice what he or she preaches!

Teachers strive for excellence by presenting material every day in the best ways to students so that learning is relevant, interesting, and appropriately paced. Your cooperating teacher will do his or her best to model for you what teachers "should be." Resist evaluating your cooperating teacher; be tolerant and learn from your mentor.

Cut your mentor teacher some slack if you notice that he or she doesn't *always* do everything that is asked of you! No one is perfect!

DEAR COOPERATING TEACHER,

When your student teacher teaches, he or she may feel like a juggler, balancing student-led learning, technology integration, formative assessment, pacing, and classroom management while attempting to reach the learning targets.

After completing a lesson and listening to your feedback, your teacher intern probably gives your critiques substantial thought as he or she prepares for the next lesson. Your intern wants to ensure that his or her lessons are up to par as he or she strives to teach like a seasoned veteran.

However, when your student teacher observes *you* teach he or she may sometimes notice that *you* aren't adhering to the same expectations that you require from him or her! Your teacher intern may wonder—how can you expect more from a pre-service teacher than a veteran teacher?

It's tough for your pre-service teacher if you insist on seeing teaching practices that you are not practicing. Most veteran teachers *know* what they should be doing but may not always remember to do it.

Your student teacher may feel as though the expectations you have for him or her are unreasonable or unattainable. Your intern would love to go above and beyond in everything he or she does, but it seems impossible.

What your student teacher needs is for you to be a consistent example of teaching excellence so that he or she too can become an excellent practitioner.

⑫

IT'S NOT *YOUR* CLASSROOM

Faith loves working with her cooperating teacher, Ms. Horn. During their time together thus far, Faith was pleased to discover that she and Ms. Horn have compatible personalities and share a similar sense of humor (they both love Bill Murray movies!) But now that Faith has been student teaching for a couple months, she starts to recognize how she would do things differently than Ms. Horn.

Faith loves theater and acting, and would love to incorporate a play or a dramatic scene for the upcoming unit on *To Kill a Mockingbird* while working within the existing literature curriculum. But Faith doesn't want to step on Ms. Horn's toes and insist that she alter the way the reading unit is taught.

DEAR STUDENT TEACHER,

The start of your student teaching placement is overwhelming. Simultaneously you are getting to know your cooperating teacher, your students, staff, and learning about the classes you will first observe and then later lead.

As time passes, you will learn the routine, individual student personalities, and how you fit into your mentor teacher's class. Before long you'll be taking over a section or a subject, then another and another until you feel like you are *the* teacher! Now your mentor's class almost feels like *your* class.

It's exciting and rewarding to feel comfortable in your student teaching classroom. Knowing that you're teaching well and fulfilling your role successfully makes you proud. It makes you feel like you and your cooperating teacher are now on the same teaching plane.

You may start to notice—now that you're an experienced student teacher—things that your mentor teacher could improve upon. You may have new ideas and a new vision for specific sections you teach that could improve or add to your mentor's way of doing things.

As you gain confidence you may be tempted to shake things up and try your approach with the students. After all, if you think that your other ideas have resulted in success it's likely your new ones will too.

Pump the brakes! You may be very successful under the guidance of your cooperating teacher and want to fully express yourself as an individual, but you need to work within the framework your mentor teacher has established. Your mentor has set up boundaries and expectations as to how his or her classroom operates.

The students are accustomed to the procedures and expectations their full-time teacher has created and they may find it difficult to change gears based upon your whims. Find a way to take the initiative without crossing boundaries or ruffling any feathers.

During your student teaching placement you are operating with a safety net: your cooperating teacher. When your placement is over, and you are hired as a teacher, that net will be gone. Take advantage of your mentor teacher's guidance and feedback now so you don't stumble when you're flying solo.

Keep in mind that you are still a student, and your cooperating teacher is your teacher. Your supervising teacher's classroom is a place to learn and store information for later use, not to prove you already know everything.

Also remember that the school year doesn't end when your placement ends. The reins of the class or classes you teach will be handed back to your mentor teacher once you leave. Your mentor would like to see you working under the same umbrella with him or her so the transition back is smooth.

Your education won't end with graduation. As a teacher, you will be learning constantly. Listen and ask questions to aid you in the learning process. Use your semester or year of student teaching to *begin* your teacher education and view it as never ending.

DEAR COOPERATING TEACHER,

When beginning student teaching, your student teacher is both eager and anxious. Your teacher intern is thrilled to finally be at the point in his or her educational journey to put new skills to work, but also petrified that he or she won't measure up.

After spending days or weeks in new teaching placements, your student teacher will start to loosen up and grow accustomed to new surroundings. Your intern will teach and fail, teach and succeed, and along the way get a feel for his or her unique teaching style.

Your pre-service teacher's confidence will increase as he or she assumes responsibility of your sections or classroom routine, and before long he or she will have a hand in all facets of teaching. Before your very eyes, your teacher intern will transform into an assessment-administering, lesson-planning, test-writing, IEP-reading, and technology-integrating machine!

Your student teacher may start to feel like a "real" teacher. Something has "clicked" and his or her demeanor has changed and he or she may seem different. Your teacher intern may feel "ready" and request more autonomy to teach in his or her own way.

Especially if your intern has a different teaching style than yours, he or she may want to try a new behavior plan, rearrange student desks, or incorporate a new unit. Your student teacher walks a fine line—he or she wants to be his or her own person while still being respectful of you.

All student teachers want guidance, but also a chance to establish themselves as teachers. Teacher interns want to show their mentor teachers, professors, and students how knowledgeable they are. Student teachers want to be taken seriously and also want their cooperating teachers to be proud of them.

When a mentor teacher sees his or her teacher intern branch out and try out strategies different from the mentor's own, he or she may feel insulted or feel as though the intern is "putting down" the methods that the intern has seen the mentor use.

It is likely that your student teacher will adopt some of your instructional habits and mannerisms but your teacher intern will most certainly try out what feels most comfortable to him or her.

Your student teacher's role isn't to emulate you, and he or she isn't trying to "one up" you or prove that he or she is better than you. But rather your intern is showing you that your influence and input has helped transform him or her into a confident, thoughtful, successful teacher.

13

FLEXIBILITY IS KEY, FOR BOTH MENTOR AND TEACHER INTERN

Susan has been student teaching in Mrs. Collins's class for a month and feels confident in the lessons she has prepared and taught so far. Susan has an idea for a science experiment using nutrient agar the students prepare themselves before swabbing different parts of the school for bacteria and other possible germs.

Mrs. Collins hasn't designed an experiment like this before, and Susan thinks it will be an exciting, hands-on activity. Susan has been interested in science since childhood and would love to share her enthusiasm and knowledge with the students.

However, after looking through Susan's lesson plans, Mrs. Collins doesn't think the entire lesson will fit within the two-day time she has allotted for the activity. She asks Susan to shorten the plan to fit, but Susan digs in her heels. She cannot possibly fit everything she wants the students to know and do within two days! Susan is resentful of her cooperating teacher and doesn't understand why Mrs. Collins is so unyielding to her proposed timeline.

DEAR STUDENT TEACHER,

You may have known for quite sometime—maybe as a child, or once you were in high school or early in college—that you wanted to become a teacher someday and took steps to make that plan possible.

Perhaps someone in your family is a teacher, or you were exposed to working with children and young adults through Sunday school, babysitting, or volunteering. Maybe you were inspired by a former teacher and want to follow in his or her footsteps.

Once you knew the direction of your future career, you chose part-time jobs, hobbies, and then later, you chose a university and enrolled in college courses that would help you become a successful educator.

Through your education program you may have learned how you can put your experiences and skills to good use—planning exciting lessons that engage young learners. Now as a teacher intern, you may be confident with your skills as a student teacher and have a plan for how to use those abilities in your placement.

After you begin student teaching and learn about the students and how your supervising teacher has set up his or her classroom, you may feel ready to implement *your* lessons, *your* way.

Maybe you plan the *perfect* lesson, right down to the number of minutes you'll need to hand out homework. You think your activity is attractive, thought provoking, and hits every target expected. It includes various components that you feel fit the needs of the diverse learners in the classroom, *but* your cooperating teacher tells you that it's not going to work.

You may insist that the standard is being met or the formative assessment you'll record is useful, but your mentor teacher doesn't agree. He or she may find parts they would like you to change and adapt to fit his or her expectations and you *don't like it.*

It's easy to get set in your ways and put on blinders when it comes to suggestions. Sometimes student teachers can be inflexible—insisting their idea or lesson that they've spent much time preparing will work as is and turn a blind eye to how it could be improved.

Cooperating teachers don't want you to feel like what you've prepared is "no good" but they need to consider how your collective choices in what is taught or how it is taught will affect the students, the schedule, and their educational goals.

Remain flexible and resist digging in your heels about the little details within the grand scheme of student teaching. Don't turn discussions into heated negotiations with your supervising teacher or start a battle of wills—you *will* lose!

Instead of getting hot under the collar, ask your cooperating teacher for specifics. How many minutes does he or she envision your lesson staying under? Which components don't seem to fit? How can you change pieces of the activity while still maintaining the integrity of your vision?

You know what you *want* to teach and how you *want* to do it, but your mentor teacher knows what you *need* to do in order for your plan of action to be appropriate for your learners. Trust his or her suggestions; the more you respect your cooperating teacher's input the more he or she will trust your decisions in the future.

Beyond your mentor's critiques, other changes and interruptions can alter your plans. What would you do if there were an unscheduled fire drill in the middle of an activity you were leading? What if a student asks an intriguing question that leads you slightly off subject—would you explore the spontaneous and engaging new direction of discourse or stick to your plan? What would you do if your lesson takes longer than you anticipated? Or what if you wrap it up much sooner than you thought you would?

Thinking through these possible scenarios and others (see appendix L for additional scenarios) may help you realize how flexible you *can* be when you're in the thick of it. A well-prepared lesson is the best plan in teaching, but knowing what to do when you *can't* stick to the plan is a close second. Good teachers learn to think on their feet and react to situations quickly and in ways that best serves their students.

Trust yourself as a teacher-to-be but remain flexible and amenable to your cooperating teacher and students. Being the best teacher you can be doesn't always mean sticking to your original plan.

DEAR COOPERATING TEACHER,

Throughout many student teachers' college careers they have been told to take the initiative, think differently, be creative, and try to see things from different perspectives. Pre-service teachers are not only required to complete many hours of education credits, but they are also pushed into courses to study classic literature, write creatively, experiment in a lab, and explore times and places in both the recent and distant past.

These various types of exposures and experiences have made teacher interns well rounded and ready to incorporate pieces of past courses, knowledge, and their own passions and interests within their teaching. Interns are eager to pass on that information to students and foster a similar curiosity within young learners.

Student teachers are finally in a position to try their ideas out and then are sometimes told they can't, or they can't teach how they would like, or that they need to change their focus, their vision, and adhere to their cooperating teachers' wishes. It can be disheartening and frustrating for pre-service teachers to hear that they can't experiment with teaching their own ideas!

If your teacher intern questions your recommendations, he or she isn't trying to be unreasonable or inflexible, but is trying to advocate for his or her own teaching strategies. Your intern knows that what he or she wants to try out is possibly different than what or how you've taught in the past, but that it doesn't necessarily mean that it's wrong.

Your student teacher hopes that if you turn down his or her idea, or ask it to be changed, that you have a logical reason other than "that's not the way I've always done it."

Sometimes veteran teachers get stuck in a rut of doing things in the same way year after year and feel secure because it has worked for them. Just like ordering the same thing upon every visit to a favorite restaurant—it's safe to stick to what you always order but that doesn't mean there aren't equally good or *better* items on the menu!

Teacher interns that co-teach within their mentor teachers' classrooms give their mentors the chance to shake things up. Use your best judgment to decide what will or will not work with your students, but try a "new way" when the opportunity strikes. Welcome creativity and innovation from your intern—you may like it!

14

BE YOUR OWN ADVOCATE

Two months ago Mr. Liu began hosting Eleni, a bright, ambitious, and capable new student teacher. Mr. Liu enjoys working with Eleni but lately he has become annoyed with her inconsistency. Eleni has been deviating from her plans and from Mr. Liu's expectations and subsequent suggestions. During a few recent lessons, his students have been taught whatever Eleni decides is important on the spur of the moment, rather than what is outlined on her lesson plan.

Although Mr. Liu appreciates his student teacher's open-mindedness, he is seeing holes in his students' learning and achievement. Mr. Liu doesn't want to squash his intern's creativity (which can be an asset) but Eleni's impromptu lessons continue popping up despite his counseling.

DEAR STUDENT TEACHER,

Throughout your educational journey to become a teacher, you have had to fulfill the expectations of others in order to achieve your goals. To enroll in your chosen college, you had to have a certain GPA and SAT or ACT score. As a college student you needed to take specific classes and fulfill certain requirements before you could begin student teaching. And now as a student teacher, you need the approval of your cooperating teacher and university professors to satisfactorily complete your teacher training and graduate with a teaching degree.

Many components of your education seem out of your control. You can't help it if your university requires you to use a lesson plan format you don't like. You feel as though you can't regulate the amount of feedback you receive from your mentor teacher. And you can't seem to control if and when you will get hired next fall!

Your final year in college and student teaching are like the last few days of school before summer vacation. Right now you are still guided by a routine and schedule made by someone else, but very soon you will be on your own, making your own decisions without a structured way of life. A scary thought to some, a liberating idea to others.

After graduation, the road laid out by university professors and cooperating teachers will vanish and you will have to choose a new avenue. Your new path will be full of twists and turns and paved with resumes, interviews, phone calls, e-mails, and stress galore.

In order to secure a teaching position you will need to advocate for yourself. Share how your experiences have made you a successful teacher. Be positive and prove that you are the right person for the job. Prospective principals and administrators will be impressed with confident candidates who have a sound idea of what they want and the experience and optimism to adapt to the demands of a new classroom.

Since you are not quite ready to cross that post-graduation bridge, think about ways you can advocate for yourself *now* during your student teaching placement. Create files for lesson plans and materials from your cooperating teacher's classroom to use once you have your own classroom. Visit other classrooms to see how both new (since that will soon be you) and veteran teachers conduct their classrooms. If you teach in a union district or region, consider joining a student education association and take a look at the grants and programs for pre-service teachers.

Keep in mind that your mentor teacher is there to guide you during your student teaching placement, but his or her main focus will always be the students. You may need to advocate for your own needs and education within your mentor's classroom by reminding your cooperating teacher of necessary course requirements, observations, and approvals.

Did you tell your cooperating teacher that you would like some conference time with him and he resisted? Have you explained to your mentor teacher that you need to take over an additional duty and she told you she didn't think you should?

If you feel that your mentor teacher isn't allowing you to fulfill your educational needs, you will need to discuss that with your university professor or supervisor. Speaking up is tough to do, but it's better than continuing your student teaching placement without the proper experiences.

Within a short time, you will likely be a certified teacher—a real professional. In order to achieve that goal, immerse yourself in your student teaching placement and try to think like a professional. Advocate for your needs now so that you can begin your career of service to students and families on the right (and self-confident) foot.

Up to this point, your educational requirements were provided, and whether you liked it or not, you had to follow. But soon you will be able to choose where you go and what you do next. Use your last bit of hand-holding to steady yourself for the exciting, yet intimidating, world at your feet.

DEAR COOPERATING TEACHER,

During your student teacher's placement, he or she is simultaneously living in the present and the future. He or she is busy fulfilling the requirements of a teacher intern while preparing for life as an up-and-coming educator.

Throughout your intern's placement he or she may go back and forth between wanting specific directions from you about what to teach, and craving the independence to make his or her own educational choices. You will likely give your student teacher opportunities to experiment but will guide him or her toward practices that best fit your students' needs and the educational goals you are required to satisfy.

It is, after all, your classroom, your students and your reputation on the line. If something were to happen—an unhappy parent, a botched test, or an accident in the classroom—it could adversely come back to you, professionally and contractually.

You are responsible for your student teacher and the choices he or she makes while under your supervision. So what do you do if your teacher intern makes poor choices?

The first thing you do is talk to your intern directly. Let him or her know *specifically* what you expect to see and why. If needed, contrast what you have seen with your expectations. Your pre-service teacher may feel put out or agitated that you do not agree with how he or she is teaching, but you need to advocate for yourself, your students' best interests, and your school.

Provide your student teacher with prompts, examples, and ways he or she can improve in the areas that warrant reform. Ask your teacher intern to reflect on ways to progress, and hold them accountable for following through.

Once your student teacher understands how and why he or she needs to modify his or her approach, watch for positive signs of change. If you notice that your teacher intern is trying out your suggestions, tell them how much you appreciate his or her effort. If your intern is effective when teaching a new lesson with your guidance in mind, congratulate him or her on the success.

And concurrently you should keep in mind the stress your student teacher may be under and try to remember how challenging your student teaching experience was.

Your teacher intern likely realizes that your students come first in your classroom. The students' need for thoughtful, meaningful instruction outweighs your intern's desire to attempt novel lessons. But your student teacher hopes that you consider his or her development because he or she is your student too.

15

ADMINISTRATORS' ROLE

Every position at elementary, junior high, and high schools is important. From the custodians to the cafeteria staff, from the teachers and teacher's aides to administrative staff and principals, each job fulfills a different role in the lives of students.

However at the school level, generally only teachers have played a role in student teachers' development. The oldest "students" in the school often have little support outside of their cooperating teachers' classrooms. For the most part, this makes sense. Teacher interns are learning to be educators, so naturally they should spend the majority of their time with teachers.

For most administrators, working with student teachers is not part of their job description. Administrators are stretched thin, between teacher evaluations, administration meetings, school functions, their own evaluations, parent visits, and hundreds of daily e-mails. Helping teacher interns may likely not fit in the schedule.

In addition, principals and other administrative staff have little to do with their teachers as mentors and only observe, evaluate, and counsel them as classroom teachers, not as supervising teachers.

Like many of the interactions they have with students, principals, and department heads, administrative staff may only *see* a mentor or intern if there is a problem. Principals report that they rarely hear about a student teacher unless he or she is having problems, or if he or she is chained to the copier in the teacher's lounge. Administrators only notice the perceived ineffectiveness of a cooperating teacher if he or she spends hours of time in the workroom cleaning out files rather than co-teaching with his or her student teacher.

An administrator likely realizes that, like his or her teachers, student teachers are regularly part of the school and partially his or her responsibility. Teacher interns answer to their university professors in terms of progress, and teacher mentors support interns and provide them with useful skills, but administrators can certainly add to student teachers' experiences.

Principals and other administrators may feel disconnected from the cooperating teacher and student teacher relationship, but they don't have to put much effort into creating an environment where mentor teachers feel supported and teacher interns feel valuable and wanted.

To start off the year, administrators can discuss expectations for their cooperating teachers. Or as a staff, principals and administrators could consider the climate they'd like to achieve with pre-service teachers in the school. They can ask for input and devise a list or compact that cooperating teachers could agree to when hosting student teachers (see example in appendix M).

Principals and administration staff could also encourage teachers and staff to create a similar list for incoming student teachers. What would the staff like to see teacher interns doing? Not doing? Items like "be at school on time" or "dress appropriately" may seem obvious, but reminders—like the list found in appendix N—are always helpful, and having a shared, visible document may hold interns accountable.

Administrators can ask their cooperating teachers how their student teachers are doing and ask how to help if it is needed; take an interest in what teacher interns are focusing on during regular intervals in their training; stop into the classrooms and observe student teachers teaching. Better yet, a student intern could invite them in!

Interns may feel intimidated by a principal or administrator and shy away from interacting with them. Show pre-service teachers that administrators are there to help—they were once student teachers too!

Some principals and other administrators host a beginning-of-the-year or semester lunch with student teachers, inviting their questions and comments while getting to know each other. Many principals provide training opportunities for student teachers. Some hold mock interviews toward the end of the semester or school year to provide student teachers with interview practice. Sometimes teacher interns take advantage of the rehearsal while others do not. If not, consider changing the date or format of the interviews, or directly ask professors, cooperating teachers, and teacher interns what they could do to best assist the teachers-to-be.

School administrators can reach out to interns and find out what their university is advocating for students to become successful practitioners. Together schools and universities can collaborate to create meaningful opportunities for interns at all levels.

For some student teachers, becoming a future teacher may just be part of their long-term career plan. Teacher interns may someday want to become guidance counselors, department leaders, principals, or fill other administrative positions. Think about offering job-shadowing dates, question-and-answer sessions, or other opportunities. It may satiate interns' curiosity as to what goes on behind closed doors, or set the stage for potential educational leadership. We need caring, compassionate future administrators as well as great teachers!

Administrators can brainstorm other services that could be provided for the student teachers in their building, or help them feel like they are part of the school by inviting them to pitch in.

Principals, assistant principals, and department heads can make their teacher interns feel useful and important by asking them to assist in tutoring after school, volunteer at a music program, open house, or hall duty between classes. Any acknowledgment by the "boss" (especially a request for help) will make an intern feel helpful and significant. If an administrator follows his or her appeal with an expression of gratitude for the teacher intern's hard work, it wouldn't just make the intern's day, it would likely make his or her semester!

Teachers who elect to be cooperating teachers have an additional, unpaid position for mentoring student teachers—a crucial role that often goes overlooked and underappreciated. For hardworking supervising teachers, recognize their dedication to helping the "biggest" of students mature into thoughtful teachers.

Host a special breakfast in their honor, or send an e-mail every so often to let them know that they are doing a great job. Any gesture—large or small—would mean a lot to a busy, overworked teacher.

To administrators—it behooves you to support your cooperating teachers and teacher interns. Your current student teachers could someday soon become your new teacher hires. You could have a hand in guiding them to be the best they can be now, so you have the best teachers for your school and your students.

In summary, here are a few things you can do to make your school as friendly as possible for student teachers and cooperating teachers:

- Be approachable
- Personally introduce yourself to student teachers
- Set up expectations for cooperating teachers and student teachers at the beginning of the year and/or semester
- "Check in" with mentor teachers and interns throughout the year/ semester
- Informally observe each intern, using no notes or evaluation materials
- Schedule a principal Q&A session over a lunch hour for student teachers
- Find opportunities to involve interns in testing sessions, school events, and volunteering
- Set up observations in other classrooms for interns and the chance to job shadow an administrator
- Plan mock interviews for student teachers
- Request student intern feedback at the end of their placements; find out how they view the school and their suggestions about ways to improve

Continue to advocate for your teachers; let them know you are on their side. While this creates a tightly knit school community, it also shows future teachers in your building how a passionate, "one of us" administrator works to better the lives of his or her students, teachers, and staff. What a wonderful way to spend one's career!

CONCLUSION

Closing Remarks

After reading this book, you may feel validated about the practices you perform as a student teacher or a cooperating teacher, or you may feel anxious that you have been guilty of some of the "what not to do" examples in a given section.

As mentioned throughout the book, no teacher is ever going to be perfect. Everyone has "off" days, and everyone has had regrets following a less than ideal teaching situation. The goal is not to be perfect, either as a mentor teacher or as a teacher intern, but to be conscious of your mentor or intern's point of view. Try to look beyond your own perspective and see through a different lens. Doing so may help you both see how to best serve each other and, most importantly, your students.

With fresh memories as a former student teacher and a current cooperating teacher, I have made many of the painful mistakes and had many of the now not-so-private thoughts mentioned in this book. The ideas and examples provided on how to remedy possible missteps are a result of having great past educators, working with wonderful teachers, administration, staff, university professors, and teacher interns, as well as learning from my own successes and failures as an educator and mentor.

To the student teacher, thank you for accepting the challenge to become a committed, caring future educator. You will be a celebrity in the eyes of your future students despite the occasional (and inevitable) instructional gaffe.

To the cooperating teacher, know that your extra, unpaid duty is a noble one. Picture a child, adolescent, or young adult you love—whether yours or someone else's you hold dear—and think about how you would educate a teacher intern to teach his or her class. How would you train a future educator for such an important position? Prepare each student teacher you mentor as if he or she will be instructing your child, because your teacher intern will soon be teaching *someone's* little miracle.

I wrote this book to provide cooperating teachers and teachers-to-be with a text that sheds light on each other's thoughts and perspectives—no mind reading necessary! Sometimes student teachers and cooperating teachers see their partnership as forced, stiff, and obligatory rather than a joy and a chance to create meaningful connections that could last a lifetime. We motivate our students to encourage, care for, and bond with their peers—we should do the same.

But I also wrote this text because someday my daughter—my little miracle—is going to enter school wide-eyed, curious, and impressionable, and she deserves thoughtful educators who will answer her many important questions and broaden her horizons like only a teacher can. In all likelihood, some of her future teachers are not teachers yet. They may be sitting in a grade school, middle school, or high school classroom, or taking courses on a college campus. I hope that my daughter's future teachers are mentored and supported in ways that will help them grow to be compassionate educators. And I hope that her future educators mentor their student teachers as well as they will nurture her adventurous, warm-hearted, and playful spirit.

APPENDIX A

Get-to-Know-You Questionnaire for Cooperating Teacher and Student Teacher

1. Why do/did you want to become a teacher? Influences? Past educators? Family members?
2. Where are you originally from? How is it different/the same as the students and families of this school?
3. What kind of school and/or teaching experiences have you had?
4. What was your favorite subject as a student?
5. What do you think is the best way(s) to motivate students to learn?
6. How do you envision your class?
7. Tell me about your family.
8. What are your interests outside of school? What do you do for fun?

APPENDIX B

Student Teacher/Intern Questionnaire

GLORIA JAMESON, ILLINOIS STATE UNIVERSITY

Intern's Name: _____

Mentor: Interview your interns with this form, which is designed to help you discuss your personal and professional qualities. Afterwards, complete the Mentor Questionnaire (appendix C) and use the information from both to set norms. Turn this form in to your supervisor when complete.

1. I am assertive   I am laid-back

◄—————————————————————►

2. I like structure   I am free flowing

◄—————————————————————►

3. I take initiative   I like directions

◄—————————————————————►

4. I need quiet time to think   I process verbally

◄—————————————————————►

5. I need encouragement   I'm a risk taker

◄—————————————————————►

6. Would you describe yourself as an introvert or an extrovert? How will that help/challenge you? What goals would you like to set?

_____

_____

_____

_____

7. Of the following qualities, which best describes you? (check all that apply)

____ Practical and to the point

____ Intellectual

____ Calm

____ Feelings oriented, like to be personal

____ Tense and easily stressed

____ Organized

8. In planning, or working on projects, I am more likely to:

____ Want lively interaction with others

____ Be happier to work on my own so I control the content and completion of the project

____ Not be a detail person and am happy to let others take more active roles

____ Do it the night before, but it will be completed

____ Depend upon the mercy of a principal or my group

9. In communicating with others, I may:

____ Become bored with talk that is too detailed

____ Become impatient with ideas that aren't carefully thought out

____ Be less interested in ideas that show less originality

____ Be more oriented to immediate needs rather than long-term implications of plans and decisions

10. When someone shares a different point of view, I can usually:

____ Find ground to build on

____ Try to see the other's point of view

____ Persuade them to accept my thinking

____ Get frustrated

11. When upset by the actions, words, or decisions of another person, I prefer:

    ____ Compromise

    ____ To talk the situation out calmly

    ____ Ignore the situation and move on

    ____ Represent my point of view more logically and forcefully

12. In considering my organizational skills, I am:

    ____ Always well organized

    ____ Usually organized

    ____ Sometimes organized

    ____ Struggle to be organized

    ____ Define "organized"

13. List the top three expectations that you have of yourself as an intern: _____

    _____

    _____

14. List the top three things that you hope to learn from your mentor:

    _____

    _____

    _____

APPENDIX C

Cooperating Teacher/Mentor Questionnaire

GLORIA JAMESON, ILLINOIS STATE UNIVERSITY

Mentor's Name: _____

Intern: Interview your mentor with this form, which is designed to help you discuss your personal and professional qualities. Use this mentor questionnaire and your intern questionnaire to help set norms.

1. I am assertive (as an individual)   I am laid-back

   ◄————————————————————————►

   I am assertive (as a classroom manager)   I am laid-back

   ◄————————————————————————►

2. I like structure   I am free flowing

   ◄————————————————————————►

3. I need quiet time to think   I process verbally

   ◄————————————————————————►

4. I am an introvert   I'm an extrovert

   ◄————————————————————————►

5. Of the following qualities, which best describes you? (check all that apply)

____ Practical and to the point

____ Intellectual

____ Calm

____ Feelings oriented, like to be personal

____ Tense and easily stressed

____ Organized

6. In planning, or working on projects, I am more likely to:

____ Want lively interaction with others

____ Be happier to work on my own so I control the content and completion of the project

____ Not be a detail person and am happy to let others take more active roles

____ Do it the night before, but it will be completed

____ Depend upon the mercy of a principal or my group

7. In communicating with others, I may:

____ Become bored with talk that is too detailed

____ Become impatient with ideas that aren't carefully thought out

____ Be less interested in ideas that show less originality

____ Be more oriented to immediate needs rather than long-term implications of plans and decisions

8. When someone shares a different point of view, I can usually:

____ Find ground to build on

____ Try to see the other's point of view

____ Persuade them to accept my thinking

____ Get frustrated

9. When upset by the actions, words, or decisions of another person, I prefer:

____ Compromise

____ To talk the situation out calmly

____ Ignore the situation and move on

____ Represent my point of view more logically and forcefully

10. In considering my organizational skills, I am:
    ____ Always well organized
    ____ Usually organized
    ____ Sometimes organized
    ____ Struggle to be organized
    ____ Define "organized"

11. Discuss the non-negotiables of your classroom management plan:
    _____
    _____
    _____

12. Do you come to school early to work or do you prefer after-school hours? How will this impact your intern's schedule? _____
    _____

13. List the top three expectations that you have for your intern:
    1) _____
    2) _____
    3) _____

14. Considering your personality and teaching style, please discuss any other personal characteristics you would find most conducive for a good working relationship with each other: _____
    _____
    _____
    _____

APPENDIX D

Student Teacher Skills: Proficiencies Incoming Student Teachers Should Possess

- Open-minded
- Strong work ethic, "hard worker"
- Communicate well
- Active listener
- Confident
- Resourceful
- Assertive, risk taker
- Empathetic
- Responsible in how you carry yourself
- Respectful of cooperating teacher, students, families, and staff
- Able to work collaboratively with mentor and staff
- Take pride in your work
- Support students
- Caring and thoughtful
- Conscious of what you do and say in front of students and staff
- Resilient, able to let things go

APPENDIX E

Cooperating Teacher Skills:
Proficiencies Mentor Teachers Should Possess

- Patient with student teacher and his or her questions
- Model best practices in teaching
- Communicate well
- Honest without being hurtful
- Positive and encouraging
- Flexible, willing to let things go
- Empathetic
- Observant—know when to step in and when not to
- Active listener
- Facilitate rather than dictate
- Caring, nurturing, and thoughtful
- Clear and consistent with expectations
- Well informed on best practices
- Present for his or her student teacher

APPENDIX F

Questions for Discussion

Student teachers and cooperating teachers can fill this out together after reading this text:

Which sections/ideas resonated with you as a teacher?

Choose an example from the book that is indicative of your personality and/or teaching style.

Were there any examples or topics that you disagreed with? How were they different from your experiences?

How has your perception of student teachers' and/or cooperating teachers' roles changed after reading?

How do you prefer to plan? Alone? Cooperatively? How is that compatible/incompatible with your student teacher or cooperating teacher?

Where do you see yourself next year? In five years? Ten years?

What about your grade level is exciting and fun? What is most challenging?

APPENDIX G

Basic Student Teacher Observation Form

| Student Teacher: |
| Cooperating Teacher: |
| Date: |
| School/Grade/Subject: |
| Name of Activity: |

Strengths:	Areas for growth:

How will feedback affect future lesson planning? (ST fills out)

APPENDIX H

Primary School Staff List

Find out the names of the staff members listed below and try to find out one "fun fact" about each.

Principal _____

_____

Administrative Assistants _____

_____

Nurse(s) _____

_____

Custodian(s) _____

_____

Grade-Level Team Members _____

_____

Special Education Teacher(s) _____

_____

ELL Specialist(s) _____

_____

Music _____

_____

Art _____

_____

PE _____

_____

Library/Technology _____

_____

Reading Specialist(s) _____

_____

Social Worker _____

_____

Speech Pathologist(s) _____

_____

Fine-Motor/Gross-Motor Therapist(s) _____

_____

Cook Staff _____

_____

Student Teacher(s) _____

_____

Other _____

_____

APPENDIX I

Secondary School Staff List

Find out the names of the staff members listed below and try to find out one "fun fact" about each.

Principal _____

_____

Assistant/Associate Principal(s) _____

_____

Administrative Assistants _____

_____

Nurse(s) _____

_____

Custodian(s) _____

_____

Department/Grade-Level Head _____

_____

Special Education Teachers _____

_____

ELL Specialist(s) _____

_____

Department/Grade-Level Members _____

_____

_____

_____

_____

_____

Student Teacher(s) in your department _____

_____

Other _____

_____

APPENDIX J

Using Classroom Observations
to Improve My Teaching

FRED WALK, ILLINOIS STATE UNIVERSITY

Teacher _____ Date _____

How does the teacher start the class/lesson? What methods does the teacher employ to get all the students to pay attention?	
How does the teacher give directions?	
How does the teacher manage the class?	
How does the teacher engage the students?	
How does the teacher assess student learning?	
Give examples of how the teacher took command of the class. How did the teacher demonstrate classroom presence?	
How did the teacher demonstrate mastery of the content?	
How does the teacher's questioning skills impact student learning? What types of questions did he/she ask? (List examples of these questions)	

How did the teacher conclude the lesson?	
What would you take from this lesson and apply to your student teaching experience?	
Develop several questions to ask your cooperating teacher about the lesson, teaching strategies, and classroom management.	

Describe how the teacher establishes a cooperative, tolerant, and inviting classroom environment to engage students in the learning process. Give specific examples from the lesson and how these interactions related to or improved classroom management.

Cooperative classroom environment	
Tolerant classroom environment	
Inviting classroom environment	

APPENDIX K

Co-Teaching: Ways to Support Rather Than Evaluate Your Student Teacher in the Classroom

- Small-group enrichment
- Homework collection/grading
- Observe student learning while walking around the classroom
- Gain a student's perspective by "being" a student in class
- Conduct individual assessments
- Gather resources or materials for your student teacher
- Split class and teach two separate groups or teach whole class half of the time then trade
- Act as an assistant, write notes on the board, pass out papers, etc.
- Conduct formative assessments
- Individually conference with students
- Build relationships with students
- Study up on your student teacher's coursework and prepare for upcoming units, observations, and planning

APPENDIX L

Possible Teaching Scenarios

What if . . .

- A student falls asleep in class?
- A parent is upset with his or her student's grade?
- A teacher, staff member, or student teacher speaks negatively of a student or colleague to you?
- A student refuses to follow directions or complete work?
- An altercation happens while you are teaching?
- A parent does not respond to a note or e-mail regarding his or her student?
- A student reports abuse to you?
- A student steals in your class?
- A student hurtfully makes fun of or demeans another student in class?
- A student shows up without homework or class materials for a week straight?
- A student asks to use the bathroom/get a drink daily in your class?
- A student is habitually late?
- A cell phone goes off while you are teaching?
- A student dresses inappropriately?

APPENDIX M

Administration: Responsibilities of Cooperating Teachers in Our School

- Be positive and encouraging
- Introduce to administration and staff
- Be flexible
- Co-teach, be a "ratio reducer" in the classroom with your student teacher
- Provide diverse experiences for your student teacher
- Learn from your student teacher

APPENDIX N

Administration: Responsibilities of Student Teachers in Our School

- Dress appropriately
- Keep conversations appropriate
- See opportunities for growth
- Be positive!
- Pitch in and ask to help when you can
- Learn from everyone

REFERENCES

Jameson, Gloria. *Student Teacher/Intern Questionnaire*. Illinois State University, Bloomington. 2010. Print.

Jameson, Gloria. *Cooperating Teacher/Mentor Questionnaire*. Illinois State University, Bloomington. 2010. Print.

Walk, Fred. *Using Classroom Observations to Improve My Teaching*. Illinois State University, Bloomington. 2014. Print.